The 140s

Andrew Taylor

Leafe Press

Published by Leafe Press
www.leafepress.com

Copyright © Andrew Taylor, 2017
ISBN 978-1-9999451-0-7

Cover photograph of Hamburg docks, Alan Baker,
copyright © Alan Baker, 2017

These poems were written between 29th November 2016 and 29th April 2017.

'Soiled by oily traffic dirt' through to 'Named tree replanted' featured in a collaboration with David Spittle as 'Warehouse Tapes' and were performed at The Everyman Theatre in Liverpool on 11th February 2017, as part of the North X Northwest Poetry Tour organised by The Enemies Project. Thanks to Steven Fowler and Tom Jenks. 'Warehouse Tapes' was later published in *Otoliths*. 'First painting is dead' and 'age the eggs' were written in collaboration with the Liverpool artist, Josie Jenkins, who blogged about the process here: https:// www.a-n.co.uk/blogs/sky-groundbeing

Some of these poems have appeared in the following publications: *The Red Ceilings, Stride, Zarf* and *Bystander* (Nottingham: Launderette Books, 2017). Thanks to the editors.

Some poems appeared in the exhibition 'Poems on Prescription' at the Doctor's Orders Pub, Nottingham, during the Nottingham Poetry Festival, April 2017. Thanks to Shaun Belcher. Five of the poems featured in Purple Reign, the sublime mystery of Prince, at the University of Salford in May 2017. Thank you to the convenors.

Andrew Taylor

For Nichola Taylor and Rachel Smith

Soiled by oily traffic dirt everyday carry tour van repacked west coast terminus homogenised forecourt Grafton Place shortcut to sleep

Shelter canopy of sorts glisten of road sheen wisp of surface uphill the fumes regularise post box angled leans one collection per day

coffee & egg mayo on brown central reservation purple pipe south of the gap spotted by Rachel peels away like the northbound track

2 3 4 Advent calendar paper bags shelf pine blanket box a Christmas gift day after tree decoration tying knots on chocolate decorations

Can you start the peel? two days on squeeze the juice for the morning / glitter star purple loom band tilt of live tree toward the light

austere black & whites / relight the tree / blue poles 1952 / reduce the output to next to nothing / thinking about the work is a part of it

Fresh coffee hostess self-serve first nine pause en-route /forthcoming season the call pre-dawn & twilight such regularity /set your watch a touch of Jack Frost to improve the flavour / over 'Four' robin song / pause to confirm decrease the volume pinpoint the toy piano

Let the vegetables get to know each other / go outside check the temperature place the parsnips on a frozen lawn think of the flavour

Winter thriller find some snow gathered in a corner of the car park the timer will brew the coffee and turn on the lights one lump or two?

Down swoop the crows / you may need to retune / transition into winter / candlelight & heat / bread wrappers & coffee cups bear season signs

Bare trees bones against the fog / travel north to get west third track of four / sweep points first valley fog lifts leaves carpet trace

'Liverpool your next and final stop' through rock & sandstone rain slashed window old footprint L2 slope of the Vernon floor cast of sodium

Airport now 24 hours! the 86 runs toward South Parkway red amber green junction shine of surface like the August day we flew into Liverpool

Blue dots on black keys red paper heart cactus window gaps between buildings a jagged light room candle wax drops a bell shaped projection

Cold streets empty paper bag deliveries done into three tier cereal centrally heated fight for cream washed empty bottles exchange for full

Cooperative retro blue green topped plastic bottle fog spreads under amber temperature drop down hill fade of red floodlight of new build

Star cutter vintage baking tray this season of travel home rails under streets four stacks four tunnels the sorting office regeneration

'Bear tracks' moss through oil soaked ballast wreathed front door second coat reversed blue towers unused skirts fan like blown stones

Steel door slam covered yard two day shutdown the stillness bread delivery stowed junction approach the slow queuing traffic beyond trees

There was also grace dig out the photographic evidence dig out the 15 year old publications warm the space the blind is half closed

Potato onion & sage loaf city quiet bright yellow frontage through the grey Berlin pipe organ reverb creak of chair creak of stool eve routine

Stuck on snowflakes condensation / while the whisky rests the frost gathers / natural sound epic space / original postcard used

Grit on the steps anticipation gate beyond the bridge open third rail moss token granite chips between she smells like a beauty counter

Clouds roll in tide shifts along straight tracks a light glare amber to the depot halogen to the right hollow echo announces late arrival

Vase of white roses eucalyptus & red berries / beyond tallness of conifer starkness of chestnut / rain gathers in small pools

Water runs through tram tracks washes away the dust quiet door-ways vacated open 24 hours 7 days a week 'take a little shelter with me'

Cold creeps in despite layers standing watching marks made on ice anti-clockwise soup to thaw give a pound to the person in the doorway

Traffic film removal frost slowly melts from shadowed flat roof / scattered prints / inside the battery lights barely shine against the green

Slither where it sets wait for afternoon return / slight movement in the trees / headlights curve up the hill / sunrise 08.17 sunset 16.02

Named tree replanted / cold soil under fingernails / afternoon sun quick to progress / from stacks shadows / temperature falls further turn the drying sheets / condensation shifts slowly / bird traffic left to right / buds heading skyward / on sill orange with cloves remains

mist is setting in / 'Living Room Songs' playing in the living room / draught and unlit candles / cables and light switches / settled down

Highlands and Islands three day delivery / under the weather? Let us take care of you / train the dancers to travel / from the cliff top

Festive herbs / Urban personal organiser throwback / the weather is coming in we're here for 48 hours / warm up with a bottle / tree sounds

The snow is going to be heavy there was a huge storm last night / so much food floating around my dash / wait for digestion and time to shovel

Head to the belly of the Kirk take shelter from the rain before it turns to snow get the shovel and salt ready appreciate the sanctuary

The square returns to itself / remnants removed / time critical transport / clock watching / chime listening /reverberation curvature dust

Water drips from sash patterns form on the barrier fold the light in make the Sunday call bare trees house drops that eventually fall

When the highway closes down the world closes down / the first hint of spring is in evidence by early evening birdsong & lingering light

Rolling Rock glitter touch dial phone a view over Chelsea roofs at dusk 828 like a bird's nest water tower reflection draped lamp evening

Dread of the fall up on the mountain winter returns crunch of spread salt on sloping footpaths car park exit barrier removed an easy passage

No. 4 coffee boxed at one ton camp it will only get colder / new car smell ride the silence to the border / with poetry & chains safely stowed

no key no return date send mail to bookstores as is tradition public service call painted horse shoe for luck we'll need headlights soon

While the city sleeps frost forms not quite silently a quiet winter music like recordings in stone churches or dust in disused tramlines

Stoke the basement boiler for rent reduction Rodney Street winter of 1963 almost finished building on the mount shrouded sodium snowflakes

dinted tin hemp moisture high balm / from bean to bar 52% / sweetness and light 4AD BAD 0013 CD 15 Oct 1990 /the commuter ferry arrives

Sunday rain fails to rout all the folksingers / wait for the turn to ice / darn the Rocha cardigan there are a few years wear left

paint splat coloured with black pen the thinness of the cotton is telling 45 due hood up fleece lined Carhartt worn in tandem over the years

Grit roads temperature drop quietness pause in traffic morning rush begins before 7.00 am 8.23 pm it's slowing main hill remains uncoated

Salt spread pavement capture major arterial route from the city
snowdrops can withstand the cruellest of frosts flowers are a good
idea

Regeneration proxy cranes fake success fly a drone north of the
city out into the river landmark signifier mirror play warehouse
steps

Days on salt wears down potholes cradle remnants traffic island
gathers autumn souvenir throwback two junctions easing down
halfway to the city

07.55 one second vocal delay 04.02 edit black vinyl jukebox on
repeat in sight of the docks the incline to Millers Bridge then the
drop

The Friday rush is prolonged accelerate for the hill / out gate
barred / pause in revolutions /45 city taillight queue right turn
slowly

Carry the envelope to Liverpool and back empty it of poetry recy-
cle reuse bring back a pamphlet there is room enough interesting
repetition

Car park twilight halogen drops angled re-Tarmac smaller stones gather in grooves / steam from instant coffee swirl patterns against white

Last of Christmas supplies / don't bring the snowdrops inside it's bad luck / allow the blind to rest halfway it may stop the draught

Bales like stagnant sheep storm sheltering birch burns best grass grows in contested gaps turbines traced through trackside growth cutback

Empty cage in field cone next to drystone wall object expect cylinder not trees on ridge angles at odds pattern against dropping grey

Seventh button is also stitched with red cotton three and seven ten machines from bales deposited in single storey units follow the journey

Ensure the drone begins with the song carry twine you never know when you may need it like moss on a roof there is continuity against slate

Hide from the storm we have coffee chalk on board branches fall
streets empty trains run late stock up on supplies the cart empties
slowly

With the shift comes cold leaning pillar box undercoat pink post
the postcard another mode of communication rain doesn't smear
the top coat

Hang the nets to dry after a slight storm lines of colour base layer
sleep system peel the bark in the distance snowdrops check the
forecast

Concrete bay X35 yellow hatching water gatherer granite chipping
shaded ballast elevation bears right 30 hint of brake unit 3D unit 6
upper

Clean mud off repair the tear candles in chapel window narcissi
peek through a trough single track clack toward line's end ghost
platform

downriver open the doors correctly the drop is considerable
culvert data pool maximum revolutions 6 tracks left side moss
between sleepers

Check hand points stone locally quarried minimal pointing an extra arch bank slope tight reservation purple pipe weave struts colour respite

Old sections of the overhead railway remain they follow the trajectory of the docks abruptly stop and hang suspended ghost like walled off

Apply the brake avoid roll back into buffers L Rifkin sign peels in winter the fire would be lit daffodils down banks north of the tunnels

17.20 ticket machine receipt trees straddled with ivy double to single track yard long gone birch behind fence over 57 & canal bridge rust

Turn the heater on blue rug white spots up here framed Cathedral steam dust cover over machinery blind half way the night is reflected back

Trees as money maker shielded from the copse between stations flatlands spring shoots carpet green B Road in the distance sandstone bridges

Rhys finds a harmonium Natasha finds her voice bring the Welsh in! 1980s apologies for water theft Ormskirk via Bethesda and Wrexham

Like a million budgies whistling the line raised their shields and marched forward with intent t-shirt wearing men bloodied and beaten run

The trolley's doing brisk business on the 10.52 beyond the bridge buds aim skyward cloud rolls in with the tide carriage settles into quiet

Sell the equipment lose the bags there's no need for wood these days empty the garage the post box has had a new coat of paint pink to red

This is not Nebraska this is Minnesota that is a Linn LM1 is this a baptism a cleansing? 270th day in the Gregorian calendar 7"vinyl single

Wendy strike the b flat suspended two dimension C no buzz wait for the Linn kick no pressure the red light is on eyes of the club focus

Purple vinyl in transparent plastic picture-sleeve [Runout Etching^^ ^^] range spans from the note of F3 to the high note of A5
WBR 7-29174

Studios A-D Paisley Park purple custom Amek via Islington Mill without sleep or food let's record sit sing before the desk boom in place

Stone blacked modern soot across the rooftops of tenements early morning light shifts artists finish deadlines loom the station grows busy

Poacher line east to south spires break flatness brick bridge over culvert water low burst of yellow track side crossing point near Gap Inn

As good today as it's always been have you closed the gate? Green cable parallel wireless fence pink hue of granite chips dieseled sleepers

Black soil green shoots still bare trees box house level crossing rusting agricultural equipment minor power lines disused plate layer's hut

Lectum spring lengthening of the days new cycle new growth birthday hotel breakfast shared coffee new building resting place seek fast train

Pot rattle begging bowl turn away the poor camping barred view spoiled benefactor's side prime real estate occupy London forced removal

It is high time to meet this nursery tale with a manifesto publish tendencies rising bourgeoisie legacy division of labour in workshop

Coil of rope heat from cast iron rest for the heavy laden light when necessary somewhere a tea urn circle of chairs hanger for kneelers

Carve it up subsidy livery change not the usual set hand it back if not in profit 1st class in the rear coach salaried board job awaits

Candles near the piano clothes maiden leans against the wall fit an orchestra in the living room record creaking piano group shot on Instax

Concrete sleeper reflection afternoon solitary narcissus mowed lawn longer light room aired store cupboard bagged for travel daffodils lean

Receipt ink fades the porter's chilled correctly though served in a pint glass ponytailed jogger uses the canal bank 6.23 p.m. not fully dark

Red chief 4016 take an apple from the breakfast table wrap in a napkin save it footpath near the station echoes yellow line burst of photos

For details consult inlay empty platforms blue support clean glass view to offices continental rail travel London to Europe passport ready

First painting is dead witness to its final moments reuse dependent on primer and scrubbing mechanics of construction words are malleable

Balcony drop condensation glass amber smell of antiseptic dust on the floor daffodils on the table defrost the freezer on a Saturday night

Age the eggs 7-10 days let the paint mix stand add blue to the staircase railing Buddha-like figures wait for adornment balustrade shadow

Darkroom in progress slight market snowfall condensation bag of picked parsley fresh coffee timer click blue and white mugs oven pastry

Daffodil scent tyre dust in alloy grime drip tap drop gutter clouds roll west to east insect highway luminosity border flowers rail clang

Scared to jump sparrow aire de la Baie de Somme 10.56 am short sleep sky trails cross further south quieter roads colours change sun warms

aire Des Haras refuel automation exit route we visited 8 months ago new species on the wing where we sat with early morning breakfast tea

Fifty years ten days on raise a blue plaque next time doff a cap raise your right hand bow your head slightly beyond the barrier is history

Sunflowers version high ponytail shoulder height virmax mesoa-merica Joan Miro Painting 1927 hearth rest memento gatherer life played out

New cotton smell like Christmas morning sun low through thin branches mossed tiles angled gutter free ivy coats storm damage tree provider

Haul along tarmac drag through gravel marker point removal eggs and omelets (sic) 1923 hardback machinery bamboo chime soft breeze required

L.Pierre Dip gullsong seldom appears ten years stream ditch cleared apple tree burn slight spit kitchen sun drench half close shutter

With cloud birdsong rain glazed tiles gaps store aired wood journeys loud gravel crunch green chair rust peel blossom hedge buds feeder full

In corners with ribbon scattered dust from wood & chips bring the outdoor in use wood make sound make heat charge devices add kettle to boil

Place Saint-Hilaire yellow curtain open window first martins arrive circle tower scooter engine pitch blue parking sign trough pansies

Leaf behind mesh frame dandelion seed scatter squeak of gate top road noise grass amongst tiles storm survived roof dust on chrome feeder

Espace sale flour dust oven heat weekend TV supplements neon red star green brand white tiled wall cable trail chalkboard notes variations

Sovam elegance economie performance la nouvelle voiture française Francine pates aux oeufs Parthenay les baguettes artisanales 13 Septembre

Clean coffee pot after use baking paper wire wool notices Garlic Mansion fresh bread bought daily heart stone gathered on an evening walk

Chipped piano keys curtain dampener 1967 sunset down Canning spare sticks gaffer strings Tom's another sunset listening party panorama

Aberdeenshire spurtles morning use lunchtime Great Scot ideal for delicious hearty soups & stews broth stock of choice oatcakes on the side non-urban field base set the recorder up sounds travel evening flame picture riverside eating airflow attacks oak matches glass glow at dusk

Mist burns reappears burns solo piano Easter week get the Canadian ready & the burner lit bunker down there's a birthday in the household

Vanneau arc cuckoo call daylight hours extended dusk house aired south facing French window reflection field of sheep water trough refilled

Ram's head mask felt clothing woods French windows field facing light feeder also offering shelter cello & piano & voice combination

Raised Matilda mug semi circle light caught paper bag texture axes rest against white surround basket for firewood chips empty dust corners

Afternoon sheep shift toward top field burn last year's apple tree warm spring cold room cards on mantle ambient birdsong Easter playlist

White pelican yellow background matte can blue ceramic sea horses white interior back wall franked airmail stamp £1.52 scratches recordings

Arpeggiator metal strings wood machines guitars material receptor scent of capital cities due north turbine spotters four in a row avenue

Seat creak matches gate creak ash removal chips chopped basket laden light through mirror piano scales repetition crest quartet cushioned

Half window open cloud dropped still a cacophony from 6.30 am cuckoo registers plane tracker frame green against cool morning grey stopper

Tobacco bale dark morning station walk Peel Session Walkman slight snooze government scheme figure manipulation train rattle 12 minutes

Lilac bursts lane gully damp ivy creep rose bud on briar tool shed door repaired travel music storage journey provider make dust along lane

Breakfast chocolate clean the pot scattered ingredients mix the spice bake the buns copper pans hang table fold sunny intervals bonnet reflect grass growth

Easter works orange piano ode some merry circling drop light tone shift fence post angle barn store passata tin storage potted fresh herbs

Morning angle overnight webs half peck of flour quarter hour to heave rasp oven must be quick agreeable flavour in the main a gallon was 7lb

Coffee cup steam condensation slip buttercups in long grass altered fence pattern solo piano photography box utensil jug hot x bun toasted

Noyen-sur-Sarth 07.05 pointless timer set L.Pierre vending machine coffee orange of daybreak viaduct restriction filter line of aged copse

Red heart cacti metropolis tobacco tin b&w photograph light fade 08.20 spare wheel living space shades of green semi camouflage protection

Avenue of blossom chestnut leaves unfurled colour escape sash frame build of commute layer of horizon dark above light dense background

In until last bus floor sleeping bag 4.00 a.m. coffee on the roof across from the station shift in light interior switch back shutter open

Compound gravelled sequenced notes pitch shift clocked off idle machine prepare to flag remove scaffold blossomed trees against evergreen

Two pot morning house blend plank weathering good shape batteries to charge jacks to raise body cut away overall part sand part cement

clouds clear west to east tidal shift beech tree angle excessive halogen tip of green lead run off canopy drop slow cast light lean fade

Extended daffodil season High Vennel The Machars solitary turbine low cloud lorries along the 75 toward the port view from above rooftops